MW01093719

WHISPERS OF GOD

Finding Your Worth and Purpose in Christ

SABRINA LYNN BLANK

WESTBOW
PRESS®
A DIVISION OF THOMAS NELSON
& ZONDERVAN

WestBow Press books may be ordered through booksellers or by contacting:

WestBow Press
A Division of Thomas Nelson & Zondervan
1663 Liberty Drive
Bloomington, IN 47403
www.westbowpress.com
844-714-3454

Scripture quotations are from the ESV® Bible (The Holy Bible, English Standard Version®), copyright © 2001 by Crossway, a publishing ministry of Good News Publishers. Used by permission. All rights reserved.

ISBN: 978-1-6642-0341-9 (sc)
ISBN: 978-1-6642-0342-6 (hc)
ISBN: 978-1-6642-0340-2 (e)

Library of Congress Control Number: 2020916326

Print information available on the last page.

WestBow Press rev. date: 09/14/2020

To my Grandma Meme...

Meme, you have inspired me beyond words in my faith growing up. You have stayed by my side in every step of life and never failed to encourage me when I needed it most. You share the love of God with everybody you meet, and ever since I was a tiny tot I could see the light of Christ shine through you. The passion you have for your faith has kept me going when times felt unbearable. You never gave up hope when I was at my darkest. You treat others the way Jesus would. You are a special human being, and I hope to be half the woman you are someday. Thank you for everything. XOXO

To anybody reading this book…

I know life gets difficult. Sometimes it feels like it's too much; sometimes it feels like you can't keep going, you're stuck, and you're questioning the goodness of God. Trust me, I have been there too. But beloved, so much goodness is going to come out of your suffering. God loves you more than anything, and He is with you every step of the way. He is with you through it all. I want you to know your worth and how much you are valued in your creator's eyes. Hang in there, it gets better. XOXO

CONTENTS

PREFACE

I wanted to write this book to share with you the lessons that God has taught me through my suffering, and how I could truly only overcome everything that I did through Christ. God loves you so very much, and I want to show you that no matter what you are going through, God is with you, and He is working out everything for your good. I am proud to call myself an overcomer through Christ, and I am confident that you are too.

CHAPTER ONE

My Story

Growing up, I had a pretty happy childhood. I was an only child with two loving and happily married parents. I took dance, gymnastics, and cheer, and I played lots of musical instruments; I tried many more sports too. I had a really happy home life. I danced in the aisles at church, played in the woods and grass, dug my feet into the raw earth, did cartwheels on the warm sand of the beach, I went sledding in winter and drank hot cocoa, I played mermaids and fairy princesses, and I had a plethora of American Girl Dolls, Barbies, Polly Pockets, and Littlest Pet Shops. I was your typical little girl! I had a family who loved me, good friends, and a neighbor I liked to call my little sister. We were together constantly, and are still best friends to this day. My family was Christian, but we didn't go to church every single weekend. Although our church attendance wasn't perfect, my love for Christ started at a young age.

Little did that child know how much she would have to rely on that love in the future. Little did she know that her life would be turned upside down and broken, and the only way to mend it back together would be through her relationship with Jesus.

In second grade I started to get bullied by a couple of kids at school. The bullying was pretty severe, and there wasn't any apparent cause for it. When I was seven years old, I heard the words "you should just go kill yourself" for the first time from one of the kids. The bullying got out of control, so in the middle of that year, I switched to a private school. Everyone in my class at my new school was very nice. Third through eighth grade was amazing. I was a very blessed child, I got serious about my gymnastics and dance, and had a dream to pursue college gymnastics someday. Everything was going great!

High school rolled around, and I transferred from that small, private school to a public school again. The bullying came back, but this time it was even more severe. I was on the varsity cheer team and doing well in my classes, but I was still being told that I shouldn't be alive and that I was a waste of space. I got ice thrown down my back, food thrown at me, and an Instagram account made for me titled "I__h8_sabrina__blank." When enough was enough, I switched schools again because of the severity of the bullying.

Little did I know that the switch would be one of the best

events of my life. When I switched high schools in tenth grade, I got to take my very first scripture class, as the school that I attended was Christian. From the very first day of that class, I immediately knew what my passion was. That year was the year that my faith skyrocketed, and I truly fell in love with Jesus. I found a new hobby of Bible journaling and I officially confirmed in the faith. Tenth grade was the best year of my life thus far. I had found Jesus, and life started to all come together.

My junior year is when things started to change. A loved one had a traumatic injury to their hamstring, ended up having surgery complications, and almost passed away around Christmas that year. That in itself was extremely hard, but a few months later my parents got an unexpected divorce. That hurt me because I had always seen my parents as madly in love with each other and happy as can be. But, growing up as a gymnast and being told to push through injuries and hardships, I pushed through this and remained strong. After that, home life got very hard. I'm not going to go into much detail, but those years of my life were some of the hardest.

Senior year came and I started to get stomach pain. Not just a little pain, but severe nausea and a stabbing pain whenever I ate. The pain would come at the most random of times, and I was miserable. I saw a few specialists for it and got every test under the sun - endoscopy, colonoscopy, CT scan, HIDA scan, every blood test one could imagine, but everything came out normal. It was so frustrating to be suffering this much without clear answers. The summer of my senior year, my mom got remarried, and the wedding was beautiful. However, things started to escalate with my stomach. I went to my yearly check-up with my doctor, and she told me that I had lost ten pounds in the past couple of months since the pain had started. I was shocked because I hadn't been trying to lose weight. We didn't think much of it, and I left for college shortly after. Three weeks into college, I had dropped twelve more pounds. The stomach pain worsened severely, and at this point, it hurt so bad to eat that even drinking a sip of a milkshake caused unbearable pain. I remember waking up one morning and the pain was so bad that I blacked in my dorm room and woke up ten minutes later. I remember sobbing that day, asking God what He was doing. I was suffering so much and didn't understand why.

By October I blacked out more frequently. I would have frequent heart palpitations and my doctors told me that I needed to go home to get this figured out due to the severity. Things became really serious. Luckily, I was able to FaceTime into my classes so I didn't have to miss anything; my professors at my school were absolutely incredible and I consider them one of my greatest blessings to this day. During those two weeks, we decided it was time to take further measures for this pain. I saw

SABRINA LYNN BLANK

a new doctor who told me that the stomach pain was because I was allergic to gluten, dairy, eggs, soy, corn, chicken, and nuts. I remember how bittersweet that day was; my family and I cried and praised the Lord, we finally had answers! I was so happy we figured out the cause, but I was sad that I was allergic to all of those foods and had to be restricted. Life in a college dining hall was about to look very different.

I went back to school, rejoicing that we had finally discovered a cause to all of this! However, my weight continued to drop rapidly, my stomach pain kept worsening, and these allergies meant I couldn't eat much (especially living in a college dorm). What I thought had been the solution had hurt me even more.

Long story short (which I will elaborate in later in this book), by the end of the semester I ended up in a Children's hospital weighing in at seventy-nine pounds and on an NG tube. The doctors had finally discovered that my intestines had a blockage at the end which wasn't letting food pass through. The solution to that issue was *not* fun either.

After ten days in the hospital, I got to come home. A dietician from the hospital gave me a meal plan to follow that was aimed at weight gain, and I completed my spring semester online as I was focusing on restoring my health.

During that time at home, I went through some traumatic events. These events tested my faith traumatically. It was at that point I felt so out of control with my life, so hopeless, and so sad that I resorted to something that I could control: my meal plan. I will elaborate on this in the coming chapters, but long story short, I ended up with a full-blown eating disorder. Halfway through my sophomore year's spring semester, my health was so critical that I had to be sent away from school to an inpatient eating disorder facility to be medically and psychologically treated for anorexia nervosa. I was in a very dark place.

I came close to death two times.

God redeemed me.

Recovery was the hardest thing I have ever done, but oh my goodness, God worked His magic. I have seen God in ways that I have never seen before, and through my suffering, my relationship with God strengthened significantly.

After all that I have been through, I have a life-saving testimony to share. I have never felt God's love as strong as I do right now, and I had a strong calling to write this book to show you how He works His miracles.

His love is mightier than the waves of the sea. (~ Psalm 93:4)

CHAPTER TWO

———⬬⬬⬬———

Why God, Why?

Two weeks before I got sent inpatient I was laid in my bed and sobbed for three hours. I couldn't take it anymore. Life felt like it was too much. I couldn't keep going on. This was the lowest point I had ever hit in my life. I felt worthless, hopeless, sad, and confused. I was questioning God and asking Him why He allowed all this to happen and why He put me through all of this. I was having flashbacks to things that had happened in the past, and it was just too much to handle. I didn't think it was worth it anymore.

First, it was the divorce. Then it was the trauma. Then it was the stomach pain, sickness, and almost dying. Then it was more trauma. Then it was the eating disorder and almost dying again. All in the span of three years.

That night at my lowest, I realized something that cleared my tears when I was praying. Of course, it wasn't a quick fix, but I have learned so much from that low point of my life. I had been asking God the wrong questions. I didn't fully realize how it all worked; why bad things happen and what God has to do with them.

But now I do.

Now I actually *thank* God for what He has put me through because I understand exactly what He is doing. And I haven't been this happy in *years*.

God Allows, not Causes

When talking about suffering, the book that I always like to turn to is the book of Job. Whenever we go through something difficult, our first instinct tends to be to question God, asking Him why He causes suffering. Job did the same thing! Sometimes, it's unusual to think that people in the Bible questioned God's goodness, but they questioned it just as much as you and I do when we feel hopeless.

In the book of Job, God asks a series of questions not only to Job, but He also asks questions to Satan. The thing is, God doesn't *need* to ask any questions here, because He is omnipotent and knows all. The reason why God asked those questions to them was that He had a greater purpose, to influence and persuade them.

Although God asks Job a series of questions, the one that I want to focus on here is the question He asks Satan (I know, a little strange)! Here's why: Hardships and suffering are a result of this fallen world. God did not intend for there to be any sort of pain or misery on Earth. When Adam and Eve fell in the garden of Eden, that is when Satan made his way into the Earth at a greater force than ever, and suffering arrived. Therefore, the pain and suffering that we endure in our lives are *not* caused by God but caused by the enemy. When Job was in his suffering, it was because Satan ultimately caused it. However, the reason why Satan caused it is because God *allowed* it. God asks Satan questions that tempted, influenced, and persuaded him to inflict harm on Job. However, that does *not* mean God was the cause of the pain. Consequently, Satan followed through with that temptation and inflicted harm on Job.

You may be asking, okay, I understand that God didn't cause this. But why did He still *allow* it? If God knows all, and He knew that by tempting Satan, Job would endure suffering beyond measure, why would God tempt Satan in the first place?

Because *God knows all.*

God can see your entire life in a single second. God knows exactly how your life will turn out in the end. Pretty cool, huh? That's why He allows those hardships to occur in our lives; God can see your whole life. He sees everything that you will need that will prompt the path to ultimate goodness. And sometimes, that does include suffering.

If God is allowing suffering in your life and you're wondering why, it's because He judges that this period of suffering will ultimately result in something of your benefit. He sees the whole picture and He knows that by allowing you to experience hardship, something even greater will come out of it. He knew that by allowing Job to suffer, Job would come out significantly stronger and happier, and He knows that by allowing you to

SABRINA LYNN BLANK

suffer, you are going to come out stronger too. God's judgment is perfect, and even though it's easy to question what He is doing, we have to remember that He can see the whole picture with His divine Heavenly mind when we can't fathom the whole picture with our finite, human mind. We have to trust that His will is ultimately greater than our will. The events He allows in our lives may not be what we want, but it is what God wants, and we can trust that it is what we need. God would never do anything to harm you because He is the God of love and mercy.

Romans 8:28 says that God works everything together for the good of those who love Him.

God doesn't want to see you suffer. It breaks His heart when you go through trials, but He knows exactly what will unfold from them, He knows that this period of trial is best in the grand scheme of your life, and He knows that goodness beyond measure will arise from your suffering, no matter how severe it may get.

A good example of this is the bullying I endured during my freshman year of high school. It was awful, and I questioned God why He would ever allow someone to go through this. I remember the worst point of my whole year was when I got shoved into a locker, I was in pain, and I cried out to God and said "why God why?!"

But then I switched schools. And I took that scripture

course. And I fell in love with Jesus. Although I had prayed before I switched schools, I never knew what it truly felt like to have a relationship with Jesus. I never knew what it felt like to surrender to God's love in the way that I did my sophomore year. If I hadn't discovered my faith that year, I wouldn't have had that relationship with Jesus going into the storm of my life. My relationship with God was the only thing that brought me through my parent's divorce, and I don't know where I would be today without it. My sophomore year scripture class changed (and saved) my life.

If I never got bullied, I would have never switched schools. If I never switched schools, I would have never taken that scripture course. If I never took that scripture course, I would have probably never found my true faith. If I never found my true faith, there is no possible way that I could have made it through all that I did.

See how that all played out? God *allowed* me to get bullied because He knew the suffering that was about to occur in my near future, He knew that I needed my faith to endure, and the only way to obtain that faith at that point was to switch schools and take that scripture course! He could see the bigger picture when I couldn't understand with my finite, human mind! He *always* knows what we need, even when we don't understand it at the moment.

SABRINA LYNN BLANK

Although suffering is hard, God allows it for a purpose. He is allowing what He knows is best for you in your life. It will all make sense someday, but for now, we have to trust God even when we don't understand. Because He can see the bigger picture when we can't.

> *Jesus replied, "you do not realize now what I am doing, but later you will understand." ~John 13:7.*

Beauty From Ashes

How many times in your life have you heard that cliché saying that "everything happens for a reason?" Well, beloved, I'm here to tell you that saying is true when viewed from a theological standpoint.

Like I said in the last section, God can see the bigger picture when we can't, and He allows things to happen based on what He knows we need.

You might be wondering, "well, what if God thinks I need pain and suffering for the rest of my life?" What if the darkness you may be facing right now is so dark that you can't seem to find a way out? What if the waves keep coming and you feel as if you'll be drowning forever?

Beloved, I am here to tell you that is false. The nature of God is good, and although the world is fallen, it doesn't mean He has given up. The ultimate goal is to build for His kingdom here on Earth and bring Him glory. He does this by working *everything* out for His goodness, and working everything out for *your* best too! When He works everything out for your good, His love is so apparent in your life that you will have a testimony you won't be able to keep quiet, and His kingdom will grow.

A verse I mentioned earlier was Romans 8:28, how God works out everything for your good. This goes hand-in-hand

SABRINA LYNN BLANK

with the fact that God allows suffering because He knows what you need. When Job went through suffering, it ultimately resulted in goodness for Job *and* God. Job had an abundance of joy after the season of severe suffering that He endured. But most importantly, God had an abundance of glory brought to Him after Job's suffering. God had a testimony from Job that demonstrates His love to the world.

Think about this for a minute; if God never allowed Job to suffer, we would never have an example of a suffering man in the Bible. We would never have an example of how to worship God even in our deepest pain. God had a purpose for Job's pain, and out of the pain, He brought goodness. Job was an example to us, and because of his story, many people have discovered how to worship God amidst their trials. See how Job's pain turned into God's glory?

Beloved, the same thing is going to happen to your pain. In the long term, your pain is insignificant compared to the goodness you will experience in Heaven.

> The suffering of this present time are not worth
> comparing to the glory that is to be revealed to us.
> ~ Romans 8:18

When I was in my darkest place of suffering, when I didn't think life was worth it anymore and accepted that my eating disorder would eventually take my life, when I thought I deserved that punishment of death, I had no intention in believing that something good was going to come out of this pain. I had given up hope. When I was getting an NG tube forced down my throat and I was crying, gagging, choking, and in misery, I could not see how God was going to use this situation for goodness.

But now, I can see exactly what He was doing. That immense suffering in my life completely changed my relationship with God. It changed my outlook on life. I have never felt closer to God than I do now because of what I endured. The reason that suffering brings us so close to Jesus is because He endured the ultimate suffering. He took on that cross for you and understands *exactly* what you are going through. It wasn't until I was in that pain when I realized that truth. Pain brings us closer to Christ, and that's exactly what it did for me. By sharing my love for Jesus amidst the pain I was in, God used me as a vessel to guide people in their own faith lives, and I can confidently say that a few close friends are believers now when they were not before. That's how incredible God works! He brings *good* out of the pain because that is His nature! He works *all* things for your good!

Through your pain, God uses you in remarkable ways to build for His kingdom. Goodness is a *guaranteed* result of your suffering. The first step is putting your trust in God and having confidence that He is going to bring this situation out for good.

SABRINA LYNN BLANK

After I realized how God is *always* working for our good, I learned that when we are in the middle of hardships, we must ask God to *use* us through the pain. I started praying that God would use me to bring about good for His kingdom, and He sure did. God works in amazing ways; and someday, when we see the bigger picture, we will see wholesomely how good He is. Trust in God; He will bring beauty from the pain.

Today, if you are in the middle of suffering and you are wondering why God would allow this to happen to you, instead of asking God "why are you doing this to me?" I want you to ask Him to use you. Because He will. And so much good will be revealed from your pain because He *always* works *all* things for *good*.

His Timing, Not Ours

Did you know that there are two types of times in this universe? First, there is a time called *Chronos*, which is what you and I are familiar with. This is the chronological, day-to-day, 24 hour time we are used to. If you said "dinner will be ready in 5 minutes," you are using Chronos time. There is also a time that's called *Kairos*, which is *God's time*. Kairos essentially means the specific time which in God acts. To put it into another perspective, Kairos is almost like a little taste of Heaven on Earth. It is also a way to describe an event or time that feels surreal, an event that is clearly from God.

We see Kairos throughout the Bible, through Jesus' life, death, and resurrection. Through the flood, and in history. And the coolest part about Kairos is that His timing is always perfect. Your life has Kairos too.

God has a plan for your life and He can see it all. He can see from before you were conceived to the life you will live in Heaven eternally. He has a perfect timing set out for your life because His timing is perfect. God is above time; God is greater than time, that is why He has His timing, and nothing can change His perfect timing except for Christ Himself.

Sophomore year of college, I was sick. Really sick. I was so deep into my eating disorder that I could barely see how sick I

SABRINA LYNN BLANK

really was. That's when measures were taken to remove me from school and get me admitted as an inpatient. When I had to leave school, I was mad, sad, and confused at God. "Why this year? I just got sick last year and had to leave campus! *Why* are you letting me get sick and leave school again, the second year in a row, to go inpatient again? I just don't understand! Why me?! Why now?!" I was upset. I didn't understand how I could get sick and leave campus one year, and then go through leaving school all over again because I developed an eating disorder as a cherry on top of the ice cream sundae of trauma. I was upset that I had to leave my friends, cheer, my in-person classes (my professors were amazing and recorded their whole lectures for me, they were a miracle during everything), my beautiful campus, my favorite weekly chapel services at school, and the delicious coffee. I had been so excited to come back to school that year to live a happy, healthy, college kid life and have the full college experience, but then I had to leave. Again. As you can tell, I was devastated.

One week after I got admitted inpatient and left school, the nation went on lockdown because of COVID-19, and my school shut down. Everything was virtual. The classes that I was getting special online lectures for switched to being totally online. The professors actually said helping me out for a week online helped them prepare for what was to come. The sporting events got canceled. Cheer ended. The other kids had to go home. This was sad news for college kids everywhere, but for me, this was the best news possible in the situation that I was in. As I said, classes were online now. That meant I could continue my full education from inpatient without missing a thing. Not only were classes online, but our tri-weekly chapel services were online as well. Social hours were online. My friends and I had weekly hangouts online. My psychology club meetings were online. The entire college experience was online and I didn't have to miss a thing! Everything ended up working out *perfectly*, and now I know why.

God had perfect timing for me. He could see the bigger picture when I couldn't at the time I was questioning everything. He knew that COVID-19 would happen and that there would be a nationwide quarantine in effect. He knew that I had to go inpatient, and He knew that there theoretically wouldn't be a better year for that. He knew that by allowing me to endure the suffering of an eating disorder and going inpatient this year, I wouldn't be missing out on that college experience that I was yearning for more of. In fact, that whole college experience became available to me through the internet! There was no better year than 2020 to go through all that I did. And God knew that. When God looked at the big picture of my life, He knew that I would suffer severely from anorexia as a result of my

SABRINA LYNN BLANK

trauma. He knew that I would have to pause my life to get help, and He knew that help was necessary. That's why He allowed me to suffer when I did because He knew that the entire nation would have to take pause too. He knows, and His timing and plan never fail.

His timing for everything in my life was *perfect* thus far because that is the nature of Kairos. God's timing is greater than our timing. Like I said in a previous section, when our finite human minds can't see the whole picture, it's hard to understand why God allows suffering. But God can see the whole picture, and that's why His timing is always perfect. It never fails us. We have to put our trust in His perfect will and Kairos for our life and remember that our timing will never result in ultimate good for our life, but God's timing will result in perfect eternal life. If God had perfect timing throughout history, He is going to have perfect timing for us. He controls the timing of the rotation of the Earth, so you can rest assured He is in control of the timing of your life. Whenever you are questioning why you are in a season of life that you're in, just remember that God's timing is perfect, and you are exactly where God wants you to be; where you are meant to be at this moment in time...the Kairos of your life.

The love of God never fails us. ~ Psalm 136:1

Courage

When you go through deep waters, I will be with
you. When you pass through the rivers of difficulty,
you shall not drown. When you walk through the
fire, you will not get burned. ~ Isaiah 43:2

You can search the Bible high and low, but something you will unfortunately never find is the phrase "you will never suffer." God never promised us that we would never suffer, go through deep waters, or have pain in our lives. But you know what He did promise? That he would *always* be with you. In life, you are going to go through deep waters that you feel are sucking you out to sea, and you are going to go through hot fires that feel all-consuming. But beloved, let me tell you, in those deep waters, you won't drown. You have a lifeboat helping you ride the waves. In those flames, you have a fire-proof suit that will keep you from perishing in the heat, and His name is Jesus.

When Jesus was crucified on the cross, He overcame all evil. He gained victory over all the darkness of this world. The trials that you walk through in life are not from God, they are a result of the brokenness. But beloved, Jesus has *overcome* the brokenness of this world! This means that you have already gained victory over all of the trials and suffering that you encounter in life because Jesus has done so by dying for you! When you encounter suffering, yes, it is going to hurt. But you are not alone. God walks right by your side through it all and you can walk through the pain *rejoicing* in the Lord because you know that no matter how bad the suffering gets, the victory has already been won! You know the outcome because you know who is fighting for you and you can walk through the darkest valley of your life with confidence that you will overcome because darling, you *will* overcome. The strength of the Lord of the universe walks by your side and fights for you. You are *never alone* in your suffering. The one who died for you has experienced all of the sufferings that the universe has to offer by being crucified. He experienced all of the pain that every one of us will ever feel because He took that on for you to gain victory *over* that pain. The next time you suffer, take it as an opportunity to truly grow closer to Jesus. He knows what you are feeling. And He is walking through that pain with you, every step of the way.

If God has won the victory already, what are we supposed to do during seasons of suffering? We are called to "*be still.*" Exodus 14:14 says that "The Lord will fight for you, you only need to be still." The Israelites clearly knew how their suffering would turn out as they went along on their journey;

they knew that the promise land lay ahead. Even in the Old Testament, there is proof that God was always fighting for the good of His people and walking with them through the pain in their lives. And as God was fighting for the Israelites, what did He call them to do? *Be still.* Beloved, that's what *we* are called to do during seasons of pain! Our human strength is not adequate to fight the evil and pain of this world, but God's is. When we walk through periods of darkness in our lives, we need to be still and remember that He is a God of victory. He walks with you and will bring you to the promise land. The only thing we need to do during hardship is to give our burdens to God because He already knows and understands what we are going through. He will do the fighting for us, and He will never stop.

As you walk through the hills and valleys of your life, I challenge you to "Be strong and courageous" (Joshua 1:9), because you know that the battles that you face are nothing compared to the victory of Christ. Have courage and be brave when you enter trials because you can walk with confidence that you are never alone and you have the God of the universe on your side fighting for you. And someday, you will have a testimony of how that victory was revealed to you through your deepest pain.

SABRINA LYNN BLANK

Seasons of suffering are inevitable. But remember, you will grow closer to God through them. He will use it for good. He will use your story for good. The victory is yours. He is fighting for you forever and always, even when we can't see it. You are *never* alone.

CHAPTER THREE

———— ❦❦❦ ————

When life feels out of control

"Okay Sabrina, on this back-handspring, I want you to squeeze harder so you have more control."

"Keep the car under control."

"That girl is crazy. She is out of control."

Throughout life, society has given us lots of mixed messages about control. But I think we're on the same page when I say that we like to be in control of things. Whether it's sports (hence my gymnastic demonstration above), schoolwork, your job, your kids, your relationships, or your parents. It's a natural human inclination to want control of your life. I am guilty of this, and I've been called an obsessive controller far too many times.

But sometimes, our desire for control *gets* out of control. My need for control almost ended my life. When I first started to experience trials in my life, I knew that I would be okay because I was still somewhat in control. It's almost like I have an internal "control detector" that alerts me when life's circumstances are getting to be too overbearing. I envision this detector to have three "levels": a green level, a yellow level, and a red level. At this point in my life, things weren't in the "red level" of that detector yet… they were hovering around the yellow level, and I still felt a small sense of control in my life. Things started to feel out of control when my parents got divorced. However, I had other things that I could control. I had dance. I had my friends. I had my hair and makeup. At this point, I had no desire to control my body because everybody always commented on how "good" I looked from my multitude of years of athletics.

After the divorce, some traumatic events went down at home. I almost lost one of the people I love most, and the divorce was affecting my family and me more than I had ever imagined. By my senior year of high school, I would cry myself to sleep because I was so sad and desperate for life to go back to normal again, but it never did. I still had things I could control, like my dance and my job. I was almost about to graduate, so I was ready to start a new life where I could break free from this pain that was consuming my life. Then my stomach pains started, and they got much worse. Then I got sick. And I got sicker. And I lost weight. And it hurt to eat. And I was severely malnourished.

SABRINA LYNN BLANK

And my stomach pains got even worse. And I ended up in the hospital with an NG tube. And I got home and things there didn't get better as I was hoping they would have after a whole semester away at school.

The only good part about being sick and malnourished is that it gave me the feeling of being numb to emotions.

That was the turning point for me. Nothing in my life felt in control anymore, and it crushed me. As I spent my whole life craving control, this was making me go crazy. After a couple of months of re-nourishing my body and recovering from the physical trauma, I realized that when I was malnourished, I didn't have to feel these emotions that were hurting me so badly because my brain simply didn't have the glucose and energy to do so. I thought that I functioned a lot better in a malnourished state. Because of this, I turned to something I *could* control; my meal plan and body. I realized that if I shrank myself through means of controlling the calories I consume, I could suppress my emotions, finally have control, and eventually shrink so much that I'd disappear. I mean, what was the point in trying anymore with all the things that kept piling up in my life?

Controlling my meal plan and body is exactly what I did. I cut back on every aspect of my meal plan, and then my weight started to drop. I started to feel numb of all emotions. I started to notice a difference in my body, and I felt as if my only purpose in life was to shrink myself. It gave me so much joy to see the results of controlling my food, and once I started, I couldn't stop. At that point, shrinking myself was the only thing that gave me joy. I *finally* had control.

Little did I know that the control I thought I had was slowly killing me.

It wasn't until I was inpatient and truly reflecting on my life when I realized that actually, I was completely out of control when I thought I *was* in control. I started to reflect back on the ways God has worked in my life, and my perspective began to shift. The ways that He has worked are beyond my human perspective, and I realized that I am not in control of this life that I live in. I realized that it wasn't supposed to be this way. I realized that I have been coping with trauma wrong the whole time. I realized that I am *not* the one in control of my life. I realized that God is the ultimate controller of my life. By trying to control my life with my limited human abilities, I almost died, but by surrendering to God and giving Him control, my whole life has been changed. I have never felt freer in my whole life.

The world was not supposed to be this way. In the Garden of Eden, God was supposed to be in control of all the Earth. He gave us free will, but ultimately He was the one in control over all of creation. When sin entered the world, it was a lot easier for

SABRINA LYNN BLANK

satan to creep into people's lives, speak to their insecurities, and tell them that they need to take control of their lives.

The biggest lie that satan tells us is that we are alone in our suffering. Satan makes us believe that everything in our lives is happening to us because of God, that we are alone through it all, and that we are the ones in control of our lives. By telling us this, he leads us to believe that we need to take control of our lives.

Beloved, I am here to tell you that is completely false. Those are lies from the enemy that feeds into his plan to draw you away from God. When I listened to those lies, it almost took my life and I can say with confidence that when I was trying to control my life, I felt independent from God, because my control followed a path of ultimate destruction when God's control follows a path of ultimate goodness.

Isaiah 14:24 says "As I have planned, so it shall be. As I have purposed, so shall it stand."

God is the ultimate one in control of your life! Before you were even born, He knew exactly what you would go through. He is omnipresent and has divine power over us to know exactly what we will need in our life to get through those situations. Before we were born, God looked at our lives and created a plan for us, and He knew every single one of the hardships that we would encounter. His plan was created to help us build for His kingdom through those trials we encounter because God works everything for our good. That being said, God, the creator of the universe, has a plan for you too. Jeremiah 29:11 says that the Lord *knows* the plans He has for you, and He won't harm you. This plan that He gave us *cannot* change, and nothing can stop it, because like the verse in Isaiah said, whatever God plans will happen.

If God plans your whole life, that means He is the one in control of your life. And He will not harm you! Nothing that you endure is too much for God, and nothing can stop the plan that He has for you. This is why we don't need to worry about control! God knows what He's doing, and He is in control. When we try to rely on ourselves to control our lives, that's when we end up hurt. Our power is not great enough to know what's best for us amidst trials, because we can't see the bigger picture when God can.

When I thought I was in control of my life, I was harming myself. But now that I let God control my life, I am thriving more than ever before. He knows what He is doing. Looking back, I can now see how harmful it was to rely on my control to endure suffering, and surrendering to God's plan was the best and hardest decision I have ever made.

God has planned your life, and it isn't going to change, no matter what. We cannot do anything in our human power to control it, but we can work at accepting it. Surrendering control

SABRINA LYNN BLANK

of your life is terrifying (trust me, I've been there)! But it is the best decision we can make here on Earth. Surrendering to God means recognizing that He is in control of your life. And beloved, God has the ultimate knowledge of the whole universe, why *wouldn't* you want Him in control?!

God's got you right in His arms. He doesn't want you to be anxious about a thing. Remember, that God's plan will *never* harm you (Jeremiah 29:11), but your plans will. No matter what you face in life, God knows what He's doing, and He saw every event you would encounter before you were created.

When life feels out of control, I want you to remember who holds you up through this storm. I want you to remember that the creator of the universe has your whole life in His divine hands and He knows how precious it is. He knows exactly what you need at every moment of your being. When you feel that the waves are getting too big, or the trials just keep piling up, or you feel like you need to take control of everything in your life, remember that you are in the exact moment of your being that God wants you to be at. He is in control; we don't need to worry.

The Lord who fights for you, loves you, cares for you, and *died* for you is the one that controls your life. He won't let anything happen to you that you can't handle with Him by your side.

God took on the pain so you wouldn't have to; you will not be harmed!

When you are struggling with aspects of control in your life, I want you to say this prayer:

"God, I am feeling overwhelmed by the storms of life and I want to try to fix them. Please help me remember that You are the ultimate controller of my life, that nothing will stop Your plan for my life, and Your plan won't hurt me. At this moment, I surrender my control to you. Please replace my need for control with trust that You are with me and that I'm in the place that you want me to be in life."

CHAPTER FOUR

You Are Enough

I can't stress enough how awful our society is at proving you're not good enough. If I had a TikTok follower for every time I have been told by society that my life is terrible and it's my fault and I need to change XYZ to make it better, my videos would be going viral. But think about it for a second, how many times have you been scrolling through social media and influencers are telling you that you need to have a perfect workout routine, perfect grades, perfect morning routine, perfect fashion, perfect body, and really, just a perfect life?! Society is so quick to tell us that we're not pretty enough, smart enough, talented enough, fit enough, rich enough, or dedicated enough. And honestly, it just gets exhausting.

It wasn't until I was in recovery from my eating disorder when I realized just how severely I put my worth and identity into society's standards.

Growing up a gymnast, I always had very large muscles. I would beat the boys in pull up competitions in gym class, I would out-run the other kids in the pacer test, and just by the way I walked and looked, everyone could tell I was a gymnast. Even when I quit gymnastics the muscle stayed. I was constantly praised by friends, family, and followers on Instagram for how my body looked. I was lucky enough to never suffer from bad body image for a good portion of my life because of how much praise I got from the body that I lived in. I could care less about what I ate because I was known at school as the "strong and skinny muscular girl." When the bullying got bad in early high school, it didn't upset me as much as one might think, because I would tell myself "well, they may not like my personality, and I may be a bad, annoying, and worthless person, but at least I have a good body and I'm fit!" My entire worth at that point was defined by my looks. My grades were good, but not the best, I was constantly teased for my personality and love for Jesus, and my competition season in gymnastics wasn't going so great that year either. But hey, I had my good body.

I had to abruptly say goodbye to that body when I got sick the first time. When I was sick, I had lost so much weight that my muscles wasted away and I barely had any strength.

Without my body, know what good was I? At that point in

my life, I considered myself to simply be a sick girl taking up unnecessary space in the world. I had no sense of identity.

After I lost my body I had been praised for, I immediately found something else that could define who I was: my grades and my performance in school. I went all-in with my schoolwork. The only thing I would do in my free time was study, study, study. If I didn't have my body, at least I could have good grades. At least I could be considered the smart kid now. Consequently, my grades significantly improved from all of that hard work. I got near-perfect scores on all of my exams and assignments, and I ended up with a 4.0 that semester. I *finally* had found my worth in something besides my body. I finally discovered that I had the willpower to study 24/7 and get good grades so I could have a newer, smarter identity. I started to feel a lot better about myself.

Sophomore year came around, and I got my first A-. I know that a normal person would be ecstatic to earn that grade, but here's the thing, I wasn't normal. Getting an A- crushed me. I remember crying myself to sleep that night, confused about what to do. I was devastated. I had put so much time and energy into that 4.0, and getting a 3.95 for the semester shattered my identity. My grades weren't perfect anymore... Now, where would my identity lie?

At this point in my life, anorexia had gotten a pretty good hold in my brain. It's almost like the eating disorder pitched a tent, stood its ground, and decided it wouldn't budge. Well, now that I lost my grades, I had to find a new identity again. I had to find a new sense of self and worth. I decided, because I already had the illness, why not just put my worth in my skeletal looking body? This disease wasn't going anywhere, so I might as well be the best anorexic I could to have a sense of worth again. This is the first time in my life when I actually started to have a poor body image, and it hit me hard. From here, I worked tirelessly at controlling every food portion that I could to maintain my skinny body. I finally felt that sense of worth come back. I may not be muscular and fit, I may not be a good gymnast, I may not be smart, I may not be a good person, but at least I am good at my eating disorder. At least I can control my food.

And then I got placed inpatient.

And then I started to restore weight.

And then I had to come to terms with the fact that I had been putting my worth in all the wrong things for my whole life.

When you're inpatient, you have zero input into what happens with you. Your body restores weight whether you'd like it to or not. If you don't eat, you have to drink a supplement. If you refuse the supplement, you get an NG tube placed up your nose and into your stomach. It's a hard process, really hard.

It was at this low point in my life when I had to accept the fact that my body had to change yet again, and that somehow,

I had to accept it. At first, I couldn't. I believed that because I couldn't be good at my eating disorder, because I couldn't get perfect grades, and because I had believed I was a terrible person, I didn't think there was a point in even fighting anymore. I had hit such a low point that I didn't think I had any worth anymore.

During this low point, I seriously turned to God for the first time in a *very* long time. I cried out, lamented, and said "God *why* would you take away all of my identities? *Why* would you let me feel this way? Who am I anymore? Why can't I just be perfect and beautiful? Why God, Why?!" I then said, "God, if you are really there, give me a sign. I can't do this anymore, and I need you."

At three in the morning I woke up to something falling onto my bed. It was a canvas my friend and I had painted a couple of weeks ago that had the verse Ephesians 2:10 on it saying, "You are God's masterpiece."

YOU are God's masterpiece! I cried and thanked God. I thanked Him so much because I know for a fact that was God giving me a little sign telling me that He was there listening, and He had a message to tell me. I had been putting my worth in the wrong things my whole life.

It was from that moment that I decided to start putting my worth in Christ; Not in my grades, body, muscles, or my eating disorder. I spent so long trying to find things that would make me worthy in this world that we live in, but God doesn't want us to put our worth in things of this world! I can confidently say that now, although I have days of bad body image and feelings of doubt, the feelings of my identity in Christ are greater than that of self-deprecation, and I know that you can get here too.

SABRINA LYNN BLANK

Heavenly Things > Earthly Things

Colossians 3:2 says that we need to focus our attention on things above, not on earthly things. This is exactly the message that God is trying to tell us! The world that we live in is finite. It has limits. It is fallen and this world is *not* our home. Because of the fall of Adam and Eve in the garden, we live in a fallen world that is susceptible to sin, pain, illness, and suffering. Another consequence of the fall was that people do not have a perfect nature. Humanity has a distorted perception of what true worth entails. That is why we are constantly told we need to look, act, and be a certain way to be worthy. The world's perception is completely inaccurate because of how broken the Earthly realm is!

But here's the thing, we were not made for this Earth. By Jesus dying on the cross, we are promised eternal life in Heaven. God has made a room in HIS home for us. That is His everlasting promise to us because of His infinite love!

In the Old Testament, there was a process called "betrothing," where before a couple got married, the husband would go and prepare a room for his bride awaiting her arrival into his home. Joseph and Mary were betrothed. Grooms did this with brides. And guess what? We, the church, are Christ's bride! By Jesus dying on that cross, He has prepared for us a room in Heaven.

He is just awaiting our arrival to be living in His home for all of eternity.

The point is, we were not meant for the Earth to be our permanent home. Jesus was right in telling us that we are not meant to focus on Earthly things because, in reality, the way people view us on Earth won't matter in the long run. Who you are in God's eyes is *way* more important than who you are in society's eyes. Because of this world, you will never be enough. But with God, you are more than enough.

The only thing that matters is who God sees you as, and how He sees you are pretty spectacular.

God's Glasses

You formed my most inward parts, you knitted
me together in my mother's womb. I praise you,
for I am fearfully and wonderfully made. ~ Psalm
139:13-14

You are so beloved. Before you were even of existence in this world, God saw you. He looked at you before your mother was even pregnant with you. God, the creator of the whole universe, formed you intricately in your mother's womb, just the way He wanted you to be! God wanted you on this Earth, and He made you the way that you are for a reason! The nature of God is good. If you read through the first chapter of Genesis, you can see how everything that God creates is "good." When He created man, the Bible says it was "very good." That's because the nature of God is wholesomely *good*! Beloved, God created *you*! *You* are very good! God is perfect and He doesn't make mistakes, and He didn't make you by mistake. He creates good things. You, my friend, are just as good as anybody else on this Earth that you are comparing yourself to because we were all made fearfully and wonderfully. You are just as good as that model you see in social media, that celebrity on TV that has "perfect skin," or that athlete that is breaking record times. Everything about you is good! Your hair is good, your body is good, your heart is good, your eyes are good, your pinky toe is good! God created you *fearfully, wonderfully,* and *good*!

The way that God made your body is no mistake. We can't change the way that He made us. We can't permanently change the weight that our body is happy at, the height that our body is happy at, the color of our eyes or skin, or the way our tibia connects to our fibula. We spend so much time trying to control things about our bodies, whether it's our weight or shape or face or hair. Ultimately, the one in control of our body is God. And because everything that He does is good and perfect, you do not have to worry about not being enough, because God doesn't make mistakes, that's just His nature.

Instead of trying to change your body, I want you to practice changing how you *see* your body. When I had to come to terms with the fact that my body is ultimately out of my control, instead of praying to God for a new body, I prayed

"God, help me to see myself and others the way that YOU see us. I know that I am fearfully and wonderfully made, but at times I don't believe it. Help me to see myself through your eyes. Help me to take off the lens that I am looking at myself through, and give me Your vision."

I still say that prayer every single morning when I wake up. Because the thing about you is that you are perfect just the way you are. God wants you to see how truly beautiful you are because He is proud of His good and wonderful creation. The enemy likes to give you lies that you are not enough. The enemy does a great job of that, but remember that the battle has already been won and you have victory over the enemy through Christ. The enemy speaks lies, and God speaks the truth. Listen to the one who created you.

Accepting yourself and your body is going to be a long, challenging process, but it gets easier. Body image and self-love can be good some days, and bad other days, but just remember the truth about yourself. Remember that acceptance is a process and it won't happen overnight. But continue to pray that prayer and ask God to see yourself the way He sees you. Because when you see yourself through His eyes, you will see how perfectly, wonderfully, good, and beautiful you are.

You are not a mistake. Your body is perfect just the way it is.

You are enough, my friend, you are enough.

Beautiful Truth

The Lord does not look at things people look at.
People look at the outward appearance, but the
Lord looks at the heart. ~1 Samuel 16:7

Remember what I said earlier about Heavenly things being greater than Earthly things? This is what I mean. God doesn't care about what your external appearance looks like, but the world does. In Heaven, the way that you look on Earth won't matter. Because God doesn't look at your outward appearance. In His eyes, nothing about your outward appearance needs to be changed, because you are perfect the way you are. Your mission on Earth is to build for God's kingdom and love as Jesus loves. That's what God cares about and looks at! God wants you to have a heart of Christ, He wants you to treat others that way that He did. Your worth is not found in your physical appearance, it is found in your heart. The term "beauty is within" is completely accurate; God even says it in the Bible because He wants you to know where your worth is found!

1 Peter 3:3-4 says "Do not let your beauty be external, but let your beauty be the hidden person of the heart with the imperishable beauty and quiet spirit, which in God's eyes is precious."

SABRINA LYNN BLANK

See, the thing that God thinks is precious is your *heart*! You are more precious than diamonds in God's eyes. Your body is perfect just the way that He made it, and He considers true beauty to be within your heart. If you are living your life for Christ and treating people as Jesus would, that is what God considers to be true beauty. Your worth is found in Christ and your heart, not your body. Your identity should be as a child of God. God wants you, more than anything, to be known as "the faithful servant."

I know it's hard to accept yourself as you are at first; it was hard for me at first. When I started restoring weight and surrendering to God and developing my new identity in Christ, there were good days and bad days, and I had to accept that I was not defined by my muscle or my grades because that does not reflect who I truly am in Christ. Something that I had to accept, and I want you to know, is that you are not defined by what the world says about you. The things of this Earth will ultimately not matter. What truly matters in the long run is that you have a kind heart and love Jesus, because that's what God says about you. I want you to remember that you are not defined by your...

Weight, grades, appearance, sports performance, followers on social media, likes on a picture, muscle composition, money, popularity, style, makeup, hair, or any outward, Earthly appearance!

You are defined by Christ. Your identity rests in the one who formed you in your mother's womb fearfully and wonderfully.

The world is so quick to make us define our worth based on numbers like weight and GPA, but remember, this world is nothing compared to God's plan for you. You are worth so much more than that number; you are worth Jesus' own life on the cross. *That* is what God says about you. He thinks you are so beautiful and perfect just the way that you are. You are defined by your heart, by your inward beauty. Don't let the world and the lies of the enemy tell you otherwise.

Something I like to do, and I encourage you to do on days you are feeling worthless or not enough, is take a piece of paper, and divide it in half with a marker. On one side, write down what you are feeling about yourself. I like to label this side "what the enemy/world says about me." Then, on the other side, write down what God says about you and remember how much you are worth. When you are finished, pray that prayer I mentioned in the last section, and try to see yourself through Christ's eyes.

Remember *who* you are, and *whose* you are. And remember, you are enough.

SABRINA LYNN BLANK

CHAPTER FIVE

What's My Purpose?

How many times have you heard the words "what do you want to be when you grow up?" Or "what do you do?" or if you're a high school or college senior, you know these words too well, "what are your plans after graduation?"

We spend our whole lives trying to figure out our purpose on this Earth. Through the whole entity of our lives, we are always trying to contemplate the reason for our existence. We want to make an impact on this Earth and do something worthwhile while we are passing through to our eternal home of Heaven; we want to make our time on this earth matter.

When I was in gymnastics, I was certain that I had found my calling. I was training 24 hours a week, and I had big dreams of going on to pursue this sport in college. I thought that my purpose on this Earth would be an athlete, a gymnast. I mean, it made sense! I had the "body" of a gymnast (short and muscular), I picked up on things easily, and most importantly, I *loved* it! I thought I would be known for my talent in the collegiate field someday. I thought I had found my purpose on this Earth at such a young age, and I was really excited.

Then I injured my back and had to quit.

Okay, so I had to quit gymnastics and take a little time off, no big deal! I could turn back to dance! That was another thing that I had always loved and was somewhat talented at. Plus, I had the muscle from gymnastics. It was the perfect fit! I went back to dance, and loved it. I had found my thing again! I thought I had found my purpose once again. Maybe I wasn't destined for gymnastics, but I could be a dancer. I went off to college pursuing dance as my major, I couldn't wait. I was ready to seriously pursue my new purpose here on this Earth.

But then I got sick and had to quit.

It was at this point in my life when I seriously questioned my purpose. I had no idea what I was supposed to do with my life now that I didn't have my athletics. I thought my purpose rested in my dance and gymnastics abilities, and it just didn't end up working out. I was confused, sad, and angry with God. I questioned my existence and was confused as to why I would be put on this Earth if I didn't have a distinct purpose. I felt so lost.

SABRINA LYNN BLANK

When I had to take time off from dance and I couldn't exercise, I started investing myself in other things that would occupy my time. I started reading the Bible more and growing my relationship with God. I started drawing near to Him more than ever before. I went to more Bible studies, spent more time in prayer, and invested more time in personal relationships that brought me closer to Him. I felt so much trust in what He was doing in my life, even though I couldn't fully understand. I just felt at peace when I prayed even though I was confused and scared. Because something I learned is that God is greater than my greatest fears.

One activity I started to take up during my time off from dance was singing. I discovered that I had a huge passion for music. I grew up playing piano and viola, but I never dreamed that I would use those talents in a million years! I started by taking some lessons on technique, but I discovered that I loved it more than just a couple of lessons a week. When I had free time at home, I would spend almost the entire day learning, singing, and recording my voice. The funny thing is, the type of music that I found most enjoyable to sing was worship music (of course)! I started learning worship music on the piano and pairing it with my voice. I developed a newfound passion for music. I started singing with friends, and after a while, I even got a couple of offers to be on a worship team at churches, which had been my dream for a while. Someday, I would absolutely love to be a worship leader. And the best part is, I would have never found that passion if I hadn't taken that time off from dance and gymnastics. The passion for my faith skyrocketed.

When I went back to school in my sophomore year, I took my first neuroscience class. At this point, I was still unable to exercise rigorously. I had always loved studying the brain (I even read psychology textbooks as a toddler)! But all of a sudden I discovered that I had an entirely new passion for the brain. I found neuroscience to be the most interesting thing ever, and of course, with my new passion for Jesus, I had to tie it into my faith! I wrote a ten-page essay on neuroscience and faith. After studying that subject, my passion increased even more. I started a faith-based social media account and posted a video on the neuroscience of faith, and within 20 minutes it got over 1600 views and likes. The video continued to blow up with likes, comments, and views. Currently, the video is at 63 thousand hits. My account gained about 300 followers that day and I give all of the honor and praise to Jesus, that was so obviously Him working through that account. I still have a huge passion for this subject, and someday I want to incorporate my love for neuroscience and faith in my profession.

SABRINA LYNN BLANK

It was at this point in my life when I realized the true meaning of "purpose" through God's eyes. Remember what I said in an earlier chapter about kairos vs Chronos? That concept applies to your purpose in life too! His timing is perfect because you live out your purpose in *His* timing.

God's Purpose For You

Through my experience, here's what I learned about purpose. In life, we don't have one specific, definitive, purpose, but God has a purpose for you. God put you on this Earth for a reason because He knew that what you would do would result in so much goodness for His kingdom and this world! One of my favorite verses is Jeremiah 29:11, "For I know the *plans* for you declares the Lord, plans to prosper you and not to harm you, plans to give you hope and a future." You see, God *does* have a purpose and a plan for you on this Earth! Remember the odds that you are on this Earth from the earlier chapter? God wouldn't put you on this Earth if you didn't have a purpose! And here's the thing, we don't have one singular purpose in life. We don't just "find our calling" in pursuit of one specific subject or passion. It's a lifelong process, and it doesn't just involve one occupation or thing that we do.

From the moment that you were born, you had a purpose laid out for you by God, and that purpose is ultimately to bring glory to God. He gives us special gifts along our journey of life that help us accomplish that goal. 1 Peter 2:9 says that "You are a chosen race... a people of His own possession, that you may proclaim His goodness." God put you on this Earth because He knew that you could bring glory to Him. Our purpose in life is not to find one singular thing we're passionate about, because God doesn't give us one singular gift for means of building for His kingdom. It's not like God says "this girl is a dancer, so the only way she is going to bring glory to My kingdom is through dance, and that is what her one true purpose is on this Earth."

No, God gives you *many* gifts that bring goodness for His kingdom! Our purpose in life is to proclaim the goodness of God through the multiple unique aspects of our personality that He gives us! And the best part is, our purpose isn't found at some point in our life when we feel like we've found our true calling because odds are that calling will change or grow. Your purpose started the very moment you were conceived. By following your heart at whatever passions are nudging you, you are following your purpose in life. Our purpose is ultimately to proclaim the goodness of God's love. God gives us certain interests in passions in life because He knows how unique we are and He knows that different things will touch people in different ways to build for His kingdom! Beloved, you are living in your purpose *right now*. Whether your passion is sports, art, science, math, building, dancing, teaching, or baking, it is all given to you from God, and you are called to use that passion for the goodness of Him! You are called to use your passions to share the love of Christ! The thing is though, your passions and interests change throughout life. Like me, you may have been an athlete growing up. At that point in life, you were called to use your athletic ability to build for His kingdom. Later in life, you may have been interested in more of an academic-based passion, like me with neuroscience. Or you could still be passionate about athletics! The thing is, it doesn't matter what your fervors are in life. During every point in your life, your purpose remains the same: to share the love of Christ.

The means of how you accomplish this purpose is going to be completely different than any friend or family member. Think of it, every human being on this Earth is so uniquely wired. Even identical twins! Did you know that you have about 90 *billion* neurons in your body? And guess what? Your 90 billion neurons are wired *completely* differently from anybody else that has ever existed! God wires you in a very specific way to put different passions on your heart to help you live out your purpose, to build for His kingdom. I truly believe that when Psalm 139 says that we were knit together in our mother's womb, He meant neurons! He knit out neurons together to make us unique!

Think of this as baking a cake. When you are constructing the cake, lots of different ingredients have to go into it for the batter to come together. Also, the measurements have to be exact for it to come out right. And the purpose of that cake? Maybe it's to celebrate something, or just to enjoy as a tasty snack! Here's the thing; during the baking process, lots of different, specific, ingredients go into the cake. But all of the ingredients result in the same purpose: a yummy cake. The cake can't be perfectly delicious without sugar, vanilla extract, or eggs. It's edible, but it won't accomplish its ultimate purpose. Now imagine God "baking a cake" when you were made. But instead, your ultimate purpose is to build for His kingdom. When God was making you, He had a multitude of specific measurements of traits in which He made you by. The proportions may not be the same; maybe you had 25% of four different major passions in life, and you use those passions equally to share His love as you grow throughout life. Or maybe, He constructed you with 90% of a musical passion, and you have ten other passions that take up 1% of your being, and you still use *all* of those for your purpose! Although the proportions look different on everyone, The result is still *perfect*, because it's exactly how God made you, and it accomplishes your purpose: to spread His love!

Beloved, before you were even conceived, you had a purpose. God wanted you on this Earth for a reason, and He knit you together so perfectly to accomplish that reason. You are here for a reason. A perfect, God-given reason.

When Your Purpose Doesn't Make Sense

*Many are the plans in the mind of man, but it is the
purpose of the Lord that stands. ~ Proverbs 19:21*

Yes, our ultimate purpose in life is to let God work everything
for our good, spread His love, and build for His kingdom. But
what if your passions or purpose don't make sense? What if the
life you live is filled with suffering? What if there's a child with
a cancer diagnosis from the time they were two years old and
won't ever live to see a cure? What about someone who is blind
and deaf and maybe even in a wheelchair? What about them?
Do they have a purpose?

I know, those are some really sad topics, but in this broken
world, there are situations like that. But guess what? Yes! They
do have a purpose. No matter what you are facing, *you* have a
purpose.

God is in control of everyone's life, and He uniquely
constructed everyone so that they may build for His kingdom
and live out their purpose. God did not intend for there to be
a child with cancer from the earliest years of their life, but
He saw that would happen to them before they were born,
still wanted them to be born, and still wanted them on this

SABRINA LYNN BLANK

Earth because He knew that they would have a purpose. Of course, that child's cancer will rob them of typical childhood passions, but that doesn't mean they don't have a purpose. Because God, through suffering, works everything for the good of those who love Him (Romans 8:28). The suffering that happens to people on this Earth ultimately *does* build for His kingdom because God wires them in a way that allows for goodness to prevail!

There are going to be people who suffer immensely on this Earth, but their purpose is still to build for His kingdom. Through our suffering, in seasons of life where we may not understand why we were born or what the plan is, we can rest assured that God has a purpose for us and that we wouldn't be on this Earth if He didn't have one for us. James 1:2-4 tells us to "consider it a blessing when you face trials of any kind, because the testing of one's faith produces perseverance." Although you may be in a season of trials when you are doubting your purpose in life, you can rest assured that your purpose is just as great as anyone else's. In fact, through suffering, we are strengthened. Your love for God can grow stronger. By being faithful to God no matter what you encounter, this builds for His kingdom. One of the most memorable experiences I have is meeting a six-year-old girl with leukemia. She got diagnosed when she was 1. I remember she told me how much she loved the Lord and how much she trusted Him. This faith of hers was more sophisticated than mine has ever been.

Although she lives her whole life suffering, she still lives out her purpose. She still praises God amidst the suffering, and the light of Christ shines through her inner being. It inspired me and many others to take on a better view of faith. This diagnosis brought people together in prayer that may have not gathered before. This is why God allowed this to happen, because He knew that it would bring about goodness to His kingdom and share His love. She still has a purpose amidst the storm. And God still loves her just as much as anybody else, because she is as uniquely wired as you and I.

Although when people live in pain their purpose is not as pleasant as living your life out through things like music or teaching, their purpose is still as valid. We cannot change our purpose here on this Earth. We can make many plans in life, but ultimately God's purpose and plan will prevail. Once the cake has already been made, you cannot go back, unbake it, and change the ingredients. God wired you in the way that He wanted you to be, and His plans are *so* much greater than ours. We may not want to accept our purpose, but we can be confident that we are living the life right now that God destined us for.

No matter what season of life you are in; whether you are doubting your purpose, you are suffering, you are doubting

SABRINA LYNN BLANK

your existence, or you don't like your purpose, you still *have* a purpose. You do not need to search your whole life searching for what your calling is; you can live out your calling right now, even through the little things.

Share the love of God with your family, your friends, maybe help an elderly cross the street. Share His kingdom with the barista at your local coffee shop. Just by spreading His goodness and love, you are responding to your calling. Your passions and situations are going to change many times during life, but God's purpose for you will always remain the same and prevail: to build His kingdom up and spread His love.

You are here for a reason. Go live out your beautiful purpose!

CHAPTER SIX

Big Little Miracles

"Little boy comes to life after a tragic accident" "Woman miraculously cured of cancer when given 4 months to live"

"Couple was told unborn baby's heart had failed, the child now healthy and alive at 3 years old"

These are the types of situations we like to associate with miracles. I mean, that's pretty much what the whole New Testament is about! Jesus performed innumerous miracles in His time here on Earth. Just to name a few, Jesus resurrected a dead man, resurrected a dead child, cured a blind person, turned water into wine, healed James' viper bite, made hundreds of fish appear, and much, much more. The Bible is packed FULL of miracles, and it's so easy to ask why Jesus still is not performing those miracles today. To think that Jesus isn't still working miracles is understandable, but also totally false! We live in a culture that desires concrete, visible evidence to believe in something. God is still working His miracles every day, we just aren't looking hard enough. Yes, sometimes His miracles appear as significant events such as a child coming back to life or someone being miraculously cured of cancer. However, that's not *only* how they appear.

Three More Days

"Three more days, and you would have been dead."

Three more days.

Three more days and my heart would have stopped. My body would have shut down. I wouldn't be here.

The last month of the semester of my freshman year was a blur. I was so sick that the only thing I remember was constantly cramming for exams, being so weak I could barely make it to class, not sleeping because of constant pain, and getting severe discomfort and pain every time I tried to eat something. But I wasn't going to give up then. I had come so far. I prayed every night that God would make a way, that He would let me survive this semester when I felt so sick and hopeless. Final exams were coming up, and as a dance major that had to withdraw four of her classes because of sickness, plus having final projects for my other couple of classes, I only had one exam scheduled for finals week. The exam was scheduled for Friday, so I had no classes or events going on the days leading until my final. I had all week to study, thank goodness. But also, it was another week of suffering through the pain in a college dorm. I was almost there. I was almost done with the first semester of my Freshman year.

Nine days before my final exam I got a phone call from one of my parents. I still remember their exact words.

"Sabrina, you need to come home as soon as possible. I got a call from your doctor. It was random, but she just has a bad feeling about all of this. She is extremely worried about your health. She thinks you need to get admitted to the hospital, I am so sorry."

These were some of the scariest words I have ever had to hear. I had never gone to the hospital before this. I had so much to get organized before leaving, and I had to see if I could take that chemistry exam any earlier so I could get going. Although, if you've ever been to college, you know how hard it is to get an exam time changed. I was nervous that I wouldn't be able to get it changed because of how strict colleges are with all of that, but I had a good feeling because my chemistry professor had let me facetime into class for 2 weeks when I was in the hospital and had to miss class (blessing from God).

Thank God, she let me move up my exam time from Friday all the way to Monday! She was so understanding and even prayed for me which is something I admire so much about this professor. She is so firm in her faith and it inspires me beyond words.

After I had gotten my stuff packed up and got home, we drove downstate, and I was admitted to our state's largest children's hospital.

When I had been evaluated by the doctors, they told me how

SABRINA LYNN BLANK

critically ill I was. My heart rate was in the thirties. My blood pressure was dangerously low, my entire digestive system was paralyzed, and my organs were failing. They told me if I had waited even three more days to be admitted, I probably wouldn't have made it.

I would have died within the next 72 hours if I hadn't have come to the hospital.

If I had waited to take my chemistry exam on Friday, I would have died.

If my chemistry professor wouldn't have let me move my exam up, I wouldn't have survived.

This was the first time I noticed what miracles really look like in life.

It was a miracle I got to the hospital when I did. It was a miracle that my chemistry professor allowed me an earlier exam time. It was a miracle that my doctor got a bad feeling about my health. It's a miracle that I went to the school that I did. It's a miracle that I had the professors I did. It's a miracle I had the friends that I did. It's a miracle that I am still alive and breathing!

Every single part of my life has been a miracle. Because everything had been so perfectly placed in my life that led to this point. There's no *possible* way that any of this could have been a coincidence. Sure, science may not be able to explain these circumstances, but faith certainly can. God works miracles in the most unexpected ways, and I had never realized it until now reflecting back on my life.

Bullying-switch schools-**fall in love with Jesus**-parents divorce-going to school-getting severely sick-SURVIVING-back home-trauma-eating disorder-back to school-<u>finally</u> finding my people-eating disorder gets worse-inpatient-SURVIVING-recovery.

I didn't think having a certain professor was a miracle, but it was. I didn't think getting letters in the mail when I was inpatient was a miracle, but it was.

Every single person and thing placed into my life has been a miracle from God because it has all led up to this point in my life. It all falls into place.

God's Way of Working Miracles

As you can tell from my story, miracles don't always present themselves in the way that we think they do. Sometimes it takes knowing the whole picture to see what miracles are there. Yes, the miracle of my near-death experience was significant, the miracle of a child coming to life was significant, the miracle of Jesus healing the blind was significant, but that's not solely how miracles work. You see, God gives us miracles to show us that He's still here with us. They manifest themselves in the most subtle ways, and let me tell you, they happen *every single day*. I like to think of miracles like little whispers of God.

For instance, have you ever considered the chances that you are alive? Dr. Ali Binazir did a statistical analysis taking into account relative proportions of individuals in the world, and he concluded that the odds that you are alive are 1 in 10x2,685,000! Just think about that number for a second.

Just the fact that you are alive is a miracle. Just the fact that you are breathing and your heart is beating is a miracle!

One of my favorite quotes is "Miracles come in moments, be ready and willing" (Dr. Wayne Dyer). This couldn't be more accurate; miracles are happening at every single moment. When you really look around, you will see how every day, minute, and second of your life is a gift from God.

God is ALWAYS working miracles for you! He is always trying to show you that He is right by your side and working on your behalf! He sends them in the most unique ways. Sometimes they're sent as a smile from a stranger, as a friend picking up the papers that you dropped in the school hallway, as an answered prayer, a good grade on the test you prayed for, a good day at work or school, or even a day of rain to help the flowers bloom.

Every good thing you experience in life is a miracle from God. God's nature is good, and He provides the goodness we experience in this broken world. He doesn't have to, but He speaks to you through every little good thing in your life if you truly pay attention.

Not every miracle is turning water into wine. Sometimes it's turning an embryo into a human being, turning a lifeless heart into a beating one, or a frown into a smile. You see, God is working miracles constantly, we just need to pay attention to the way that He is working in our lives.

My challenge for you is to be more alert to God's miracles in your own life. At the end of your day, do some journaling; write down the things in your day that went well, and the things that maybe didn't go so well. Try to pick out at least one miracle per day, write it down on a tiny slip of paper, and place it into a jar. After a year goes by, go through the jar and see just how innumerous His miracles are! This will help you see that miracles ARE still being performed, and you will develop the habit of seeking out those moments in your life. Remember, they are God's little whispers that He is right there with you.

I want you to remember that God is performing miracles in your life every day, and He is going to perform more. Big or small, He is there. He shows you in His little ways that He is always working for your good.

CHAPTER SEVEN

Strong Enough

I can do all things through Christ who strengthens me. ~ Philippians 4:13

G rowing up an athlete, I had always been tough. When I got injured I pushed through it and continued to train, and when I felt fatigued I would exert myself even harder. I was always told in my athletics that I was supposed to be strong and push through the pain. I was even condemned for showing emotion, and that was just the normalcy of athletics!

When my parents got divorced, I told myself it didn't hurt. I wanted to be fine. And even if I didn't exactly feel fine, I pushed through it. I was strong. I grew up as an athlete. I practically had a Ph.D. in personal perseverance. Through that whole process, I remained strong and positive. I hung out with my friends as usual. When teachers, friends, or family members asked if I was okay I would say "of course! I'm more than okay!" Even if maybe I didn't feel okay. I cried sometimes, but I got yelled at by a loved one for showing those emotions. I then decided that I could no longer show emotion. I really had to kick my strength into high gear. If I faked it, maybe I could convince myself that I was actually okay.

And I did for quite a while.

When I started to get sick during my freshman year, I told myself I was fine. I didn't feel any symptoms. I hated having negative attention to myself and I wanted to prove to everyone that I was perfect. I pushed through. I focused on my grades, friends, and dance. I may have fallen asleep those nights crying, but I was strong. I could do this. I could get better on my own and I didn't need help.

The same thing happened with my eating disorder. Once I got sick the second time, that's when I seriously started to push beyond my threshold. There was no way that I could have been sick another time or have an actual eating disorder, no way. I was determined to prove to everyone that I was strong enough to overcome my eating disorder on my own. I wanted to prove that I was just fine and that I was doing it and getting better all by myself. Once I grasped this mentality, the high-functioning anxiety began. My grades dramatically improved because all my energy came from my stress hormones. My athletic performance

SABRINA LYNN BLANK

was better than ever. I dove full force into all things that could make me perfect and strong. Nobody had any reason to suspect I was struggling, which is how I wanted it.

But the more I pushed, the more I struggled. The sicker I became. I felt so isolated, alone, and sad. I convinced myself that I was strong and happy because I was so perfect on the outside to everyone else when on the inside I was literally dying. I had been lying to myself for so long telling myself my strength was pulling me through this eating disorder when really my liver was failing, my kidneys were shutting down, and my heart was getting weaker by the day.

When I reached this low point, I realized that relying on my own strength was slowly killing me. I realized how sick I was and that if I kept trying to "be strong" and push through in life I would end up dying. I knew I needed help, and I needed a higher power to give me strength. That higher power was God.

You see, if we continue to rely on our human strength, we will eventually run out of fuel. We will collapse under the pressure because our strength is not enough to get us through the storms of life. We live in a fallen world, and this Earthly realm is full of hardships, struggle, and evil. Those forces are far too great for our human power to endure. On top of those struggles, satan is constantly trying to sneak lies into our head telling us that we are going to crash under the pressure. It's far too much for us to take on alone; but it isn't too hard for us to take on with God, because "With man, it is impossible. But with God, all things are possible" (Mark 10:27)

When we try to push through our weakness and pain using our own strength, we aren't going to succeed. But God is a power greater than all of the universe. *His* strength is enough! Everything we encounter in life is possible with the Lord because He has *overcome* the whole world (John 16:33). His power is going to bring you out of trials, and we need to surrender to that power. The only way to obtain that Godly power is to surrender your human ability and admit to your weakness. Your weakness does not scare God. He isn't mad or upset with you when you're feeling weak. It's in our weakest points in which God does His best work because when we are at our weakest, and we are suffering the hardest, that's when we realize how much we need a savior. That's when our relationship with God becomes more intimate and truly flourishes. God's power is made *perfect* in weakness (2 Corinthians 12:9-10)! It is in our weakness when our lives change. It's in our weakness when God's power testifies to His goodness. It's in our weakness when we realize how much we need Him and that we cannot survive this world without His strength; the way to do this and obtain this strength is to surrender.

For the longest time, I didn't want to admit I was struggling and weak. When I finally hit my low point and surrendered to God and told Him how weak and hurt I was, that's when my life changed forever. I started relying on God for my strength, not myself. My life started to take off. My health was restored, mentally, and physically. Whenever I face trials I can now confidently say that my outlook has completely changed. In adversity, I can walk through the trial with confidence because I know that this suffering will not hurt me; I can see the suffering as an opportunity for my relationship with God to grow. I can see the situation as a blessing because I know that if I rely on His power and strength, the victory is there. I am now able to understand that I can do literally *all* things through Christ who gives me strength (Philippians 4:13)! And so can you! He died for *you!* By dying on the cross, God overcame this world. By overcoming this world, He was able to overcome all evil, sin, death, and suffering. He won this victory over satan. The power of God is incredible! The same power that constructed the Earth, performs miracles, rose from the dead and governs the entire universe lives in YOU! That power is *more* than enough to win the battles that you endure in life! The victory has already been won! By surrendering our strength to God, we can grow our relationship with Jesus significantly and truly be confident in the fact that Jesus will fight this battle for us and give us the strength we need.

Think of it this way. You are a piece of coal (I know, weird way to think of yourself)! If we listen to those lies of the enemy and try to use our strength to fight the battles in our life, under the pressure we are going to crumble into ashes because that's what coal does under pressure. But if we rely on the strength of Jesus, we not only will come out of this pressure with victory, but we will come out even stronger! Through using God's strength amidst adversity, we won't crumble into ashes, but we will be transformed into a diamond. Because His power is made *perfect* in our weakness, and what's more perfect than a diamond that God made?!

Beloved, you are strong enough to face any challenge you face in life because you have the God of the universe giving you that strength. Your strength alone is not sufficient enough to carry you through suffering, but the God who created the universe gave you His strength. With that strength, anything, anything, *anything,* is possible! Your strength will be transformed by surrendering your need for a savior. That savior wants a relationship with you, and sometimes it takes suffering to realize that because He endured the ultimate suffering so you wouldn't have to.

CHAPTER EIGHT

You Are Gold

If you've ever read the book of Job in the Bible, you'll know that he went through some serious troubles in his life. If you haven't, I'll give you a brief rundown of his story. Job was removed of all of his possessions, his entire family died, and to top it all off, he was struck with boils and his health quickly declined. If you're cringing right now, trust me, so am I. I can't even imagine what pain Job must have been in after all that he went through. Nevertheless, Job *still* worshipped the Lord amidst his trials.

Job 23:10 says that "When He has tested me, I will come forth as gold."

Job is speaking here, and he has some serious insight into his suffering. Job knew that he was gold! This is why understanding this verse is so significant:

Have you ever seen a purified piece of gold in real life? I have, and it is *stunning*. It is shiny, sparkly, and smooth. Gold can be made into jewelry, decorations, vases, and so much more. The cool thing about gold is that it can be molded into pretty much anything! However, for it to be turned into something like an earring, it has to go through a process called purification. Before purification, gold is covered in black filth and rust. It looks nothing like gold! Usually, it is in some sort of spherical shape with uneven edges. It is not very pleasant to look at. How does gold go from being a black chunky object to something so shiny?

Purification.

In purification, that original, black piece of gold gets put through the fire. I'm not talking about your average bonfire you'd start outside to roast some marshmallows on, I'm talking about some seriously *hot* and intense fire. Once the gold has remained in the fire for a while, it comes out shiny and sparkly. Also, it comes out *malleable*, which means it can be bent into pretty much anything! It's in that moment right after purification when the gold gets turned into jewelry or vases or a shiny statue or decoration. But for *any* of those items to be made, the gold has to first go through some serious fire.

SABRINA LYNN BLANK

This is what Job was talking about! In the pit of his suffering, he knew that *he* was gold. He said those words because he knew exactly how gold purification goes, and he knew what God would do with him amidst his trials. He knew God would purify him like gold. He knew that being in the pit of his suffering just meant that he was going to come out of the other side of this trial made new and more beautiful than ever before. He knew that God was in the process of molding him into something greater than ever because he is gold and that's how purification works. God knows what He is doing. Although it hurt God to see Job go through this, this is why He allowed him to go through the fire because He knew from the beginning that by allowing Job to go through this fire, He would mold him into something more pure and beautiful, and Job would come out stronger than ever before. But Job could only obtain that new beauty if he went through the fire first.

In life, we are going to encounter situations where we feel like we are in the pit of fire. And not the happy marshmallow-ey kind like I said earlier. There are going to be times we are burning up and life seems to be too much to handle. Sometimes you're just so entrenched with flames that you can't even imagine what the cool air and blue skies feel like.

Suffering in life feels this way.

But remember, you are gold.

Yes, you may be in the fire now. You may be in the pit of your suffering and you may feel as if you hit rock bottom so hard that you've found yourself in the flames. But remember how gold is purified. Being in the flames now means that when you come out, you are going to be formed into something more beautiful than you ever have before. You are going to be stronger, gleaming, and more full of life than ever. You actually *need* this fire to make you new and moldable. God can only mold you into the thing that He desires if you are willing to go through that fire first; you need to walk through this fire to let God work His magic.

When I was at my lowest point, I would have never expected to be where I am today. When I was at my lowest point, I had accepted the fact that I was going to die. I felt hopeless and I was trying everything to get out of this pain and I just couldn't. Little did I know how strong I would become after all that I endured in my life. Sometimes, it takes walking through the fire and coming out the other side in order to see how you have been molded, which is what happened to me. Looking back, I can see exactly how God has taken me from the fire and formed me into something more beautiful than ever, even when I was losing hope not long ago.

Beloved, today, if you can't take the suffering anymore and you feel like you are in the middle of the fire, I want you to trust

SABRINA LYNN BLANK

that the Lord is going to take you and mold you into something more extravagant than ever. You are simply just being purified. I know it's hard to see right now, but trust me, and trust God, you are going to make it.

You are Gold.

CHAPTER NINE

Doing a new thing

Behold, I am doing a new thing. Do you not perceive it? I will make a way in the wilderness and rivers in the desert. ~ Isaiah 43:19

When I was at my sickest, I was told by a handful of people that the reason I was sick is because I had too much sin on my heart. I was told that because I hadn't repented my sins, the reason that I was sick was because God was mad at me.

This broke my heart. My whole life I had put my trust in the Lord, prayed, and loved Him. Sure, there's been many times in which I questioned His goodness, but I always ended up praising Him more after the storms of life than ever before. I was faithful. Why would God allow these things in my life because of my sins? I prayed for forgiveness every night, so why would He still condemn me for my sins?

Let me tell you, it took a lot of praying, reading scripture, and talking with loved ones and spiritual role models to come to terms with the fact that this was completely false! God was *not* punishing me for the sins on my heart. The suffering that I endured was *not* a result of the bad things that I had done in my life, because God makes all things new. Unfortunately, those individuals that told me those things simply misrepresented Christianity. I am not upset with them at all, but accepting that they weren't properly representing God helped me better understand the situation.

Beloved, your past does *not* define you. Yes, we all sin. It's human nature because of the fall. But just because we have sinned does not mean that God is going to punish us or hurt us. Instead, Jesus Himself endured the ultimate punishment on the cross so we *don't have to.* He took on all of the punishments imaginable for our sins because He loves us so much that He wanted us to have eternal life. By dying on the cross, He made *all* things new. God sent His Son to the Earth to save us so we wouldn't have to suffer! Beloved, *all* things are made new through Him!

Before you were even born, God knew exactly what sins you would do and exactly what mistakes you would make. He could have chosen not to create you after seeing all that you have done in your lifespan. But guess what? He still put you on this Earth.

Not only did He still create you, but He still *died* for you! He still chose to take on that cross to save you and to give you the life you deserve. A life of newness and freedom from bondage.

Through Him, you are made new. There is nothing in your past, present, or future that was not crucified with Jesus. When Christ was crucified, so was your sin. No matter where you are in your life, there is always an opportunity to be made new by remembering this. The old you had been crucified with Christ, and now Christ lives in you (Galatians 2:20).

On the cross, He made all things new. Your past sin does not define you. Your past sin does not determine the way God treats you now. So beloved, remember that no matter what your past held, you are made new, and God died for you. The good, the bad, and the ugly. You are worth it.

Making a way

Have you ever seen those cartoons of a little demon sitting on one side of somebody's shoulder, and a little angel sitting on another's shoulder? That's what having an eating disorder is like. Having an eating disorder is like having that little angel talking to you (which represents yourself), but having that little demon overpower her and scream at you. And every time you listen to that demon, his voice gets louder, and the angel's voice gets quieter until her voice simply turns into a small whisper that you can't even hear anymore. Having an eating disorder overpowers your brain like nothing else. It's not fun, and it's really, *really* scary.

As the eating disorder got stronger and stronger in my life, my own voice got quieter. It's almost like my personality as a whole just exited my body for a while and the eating disorder took over. I was completely controlled by it, and I felt so stuck. As I got deeper and deeper into it, the harder it became to get out. This voice overpowered everything in my life. It got so bad that I couldn't even take a step without thinking "that's another .5 calorie burned." I couldn't look at myself without finding at least five flaws. I didn't know who I was anymore. It was sad, and the scariest part was that it wasn't my fault. I didn't ask for this, and this disease took everything from me.

SABRINA LYNN BLANK

I felt so stuck when I was at my worst. I felt hopeless and like a lost cause. This disease was taking over my life day by day and it seemed impossible to get rid of it. I was stuck in a cage that was slowly killing me and the cage seemed to get smaller and smaller as I tried to push harder and harder. I honestly saw no way out and I accepted the fact that I would either live my whole life with this terrible disease or I would die from it. I was in a really dark place with no exit at the time.

Then, I turned to Jesus. I turned to prayer. I turned to grace. I realized how mighty His power is. As I did with my strength and control, I had to surrender my recovery to Him. I had to put so much trust into His plan for my life because you know what? God makes all things new. He does new things every day, hour, minute, and second. He makes *rivers* in the *desert*! When He was crucified, so was my eating disorder. I had to realize how truly incredible His power is. I had to take a leap of faith. I had to trust in His plan that He would make a way for me. And oh my goodness, He sure did! In His perfect timing, I found my recovery and I got my life back. I can confidently say that now, I am the happiest I have been in probably my whole life, and it's only because of what He has done for me. It's only because He made a way for me. He broke the chains of my disease that were controlling me. I couldn't have done it on my own; I *needed* Jesus. I never could have imagined myself being in this spot in my life… ever. It's only because of His mighty power in which I was able to be made new.

After I found my life again, I have never been stronger. I feel like I have been transformed into something even more beautiful than ever before. In recovery, lots of people try to tell you to find the person that you were before your eating disorder; and in life, if you go through suffering, many people will tell you that you need to go back to the way things were. But beloved, that's just not how Jesus works. Through your pain, He is going to make a way. And through that way, you are going to be made new. You are going to have the spirit of the Lord in you. God is going to transform you into something more beautiful than ever because He takes what's broken and makes it beautiful. You are like a caterpillar. And God is going to transform you into a butterfly. So no, things will not go back to the way they were before your brokenness. You are not meant to be a caterpillar forever. Instead, they are going to be better. You are going to bloom into a beautiful butterfly. God does something *new* with you. He does something *good* with you. He does something *beautiful* with you. Because if anyone is in Christ, they are a *new* creation (2 Corinthians 5:17).

God's power is mightier than all. He is going to break all the chains in your life and give you freedom from your past, your sins, and your suffering. That's how mighty His power is. Where

SABRINA LYNN BLANK

the spirit of the Lord is, there is freedom (2 Corinthians 3:17). Freedom from everything holding you down and holding you back from living the life that God planned for you. Freedom from an eating disorder. Freedom from depression, anxiety, addiction, bad habits, mental illness, feelings of worthlessness, and freedom from the enemy. When God was crucified, so were all of your sins, heartaches, and tears. God is making a way for you. He is making all things new and He does new things every single moment.

Precious as Earth

Think about this. God created the world in seasons; there's fall when things pass away and go into hibernation. There's winter when everything is at a standstill and we can just reflect on the beauty of the stillness. There's spring when everything beautifully blooms, and everything is new. And there's summer when everyone can enjoy the new Earth that has emerged from the blooming of spring.

God did this for a reason. In life, you are going to have seasons like fall. Things in your life, like the leaves, are going to pass away. Things in your life are going to crumble under your feet and hide. You are also going to have seasons like winter. Things in your life are going to be at a standstill, and you won't know when the sun will shine again, but you trust God that it will come. And then, you will have a season like spring. Everything beautiful is going to bloom and emerge in your life like never before. The flowers will blossom, the leaves will bud, and the critters will wake up and come alive. Then the season of summer in your life will come, and you will be able to rejoice in the beauty that has emerged in your life. Do you know what else is cool? God does this with the Earth. The Earth is 70% water. And you? Your body? You are 70% water as well. How many days did God create the Earth in? 7 (Genesis 1). What is God?

SABRINA LYNN BLANK

The living water (John 7). Beloved, God views you as precious as the Earth. He designed you this way for a reason; He is trying to show you something through the Earth, something wonderful. God does a new, beautiful thing with the seasons every year, so what makes you believe that He won't do the same with the seasons of your life?

Take notice of this, too.

1. The flowers of spring can't bloom without a harsh winter beforehand.
2. After the harsh winter, the flowers bloom differently *every* time.
3. The leaves of fall may be dying, but it's beautiful.
4. No matter how harsh the winter was before, the flowers always bloom as beautiful as ever.

God considers you as precious as the earth; He knows what He's doing. When you go through storms in your life like a harsh winter, God is going to use that to foster the bloom of the flowers of spring in your life. And the best part, they will be different in their own beautiful way *every* single time. Sometimes, you will have to grieve the loss of something of the past, like the leaves falling in autumn. For me, it was my eating disorder. As crazy as it sounds, the illness gave me a sense of comfort amidst the storm, but I knew deep in my heart it was drawing me further and further away from the life that God had planned for me. Saying goodbye to the disease was the hardest, yet most beautiful decision I have ever made. And now the flowers in my life have bloomed more than they ever have before. You see, when you have to say goodbye to the past, it's hard, but at the same time, it's beautiful. Just like the leaves that pass away in fall. In the process of death, they emit a beautiful, unique color. That beauty is a sign of growth as the pain of your past is dying. Once the old has passed away, you've surrendered, and you're allowing God to work His mighty power in your life, there are going to be storms as you grasp the concept of everything as a whole. To keep the fight up through the winter and keep surrendering the control of your life is going to be hard. But the best part is, during that suffering, you can walk with confidence knowing what is next. By saying goodbye to the old, trudging through the deep waters, the snow, and the storms, and allowing God to transform you into a new creation, you are sure to bloom into a beautiful creation that you have never been before. And after you have been made new, you can rejoice in the season of summer and embrace the new person in Christ you are.

Isn't that cool?! The way the Earth's seasons are constructed isn't by mistake. God created the universe the way it is for a reason. He gives us little signs *everywhere* to show us how His mighty power and love work! All we have to do is look hard

SABRINA LYNN BLANK

enough, and we will see them. Things in the Bible match up with the way that the world works. A coincidence? I think not. Think about it for a second. Every time it rains and storms, the grass grows greener, healthier, and comes to life more. 1 Peter 5:10 says that "after you have suffered a little while (like the grass), the God of grace will restore you" (and make you bloom even stronger than before). Even with seasons in general; there's a time for cold, warm, spring, and fall, and Ecclesiastes 3:1-8 says that there is a season for everything... to plant, die, and be born. See? God is *literally* manifesting Himself through the Earth! Isn't that the coolest thing?!

Beloved, God created you, sent His Son to the Earth, and was crucified for you. He loves you and wants you to know how much you are loved and how you are made new by His love and mercy. He communicates with us through the Earth and His Word to show you the beautiful creation you will become after the season of surrendering, saying goodbye to your past, suffering, and letting go. Your past doesn't define you. No matter how stuck you feel right now in your life, this is not the end. If you feel like you can't get out of the place you are in, I want you to know that is not true. God makes a way for you no matter what. He makes all things new.

Every day, when the sun rises and sets, that is an opportunity to surrender to Christ and be made new. Every hour is an opportunity to surrender. Every minute is an opportunity. Every moment is an opportunity.

No matter what you are struggling with today, I want you to remember how incredible God's power is. You are not finished fighting this battle. God is not done with you; the victory is yours. Trust in the power of God, and surrender to His love.

You are as precious as the Earth. The flowers of your life are going to bloom in no time. Be still, and remember that HE is God. His timing is perfect, and His work is endless. Be sure to listen to those whispers.

XOXO

SABRINA LYNN BLANK

CPSIA information can be obtained
at www.ICGtesting.com
Printed in the USA
LVHW090224221020
669499LV00007B/197

9 781664 203419